My sister was the inspiration for me to write this bo[...]
First draft written - Oct 6t[...]

30 DAYS
to Bring You Back

GERMAINE LOUISE

This book provides you with 30 daily steps, and ideally aims for you to carry them out over the course of a month. This is in an inspirational exercise to help you get back that feeling and sense of fulfillment.

Balboa Press books may be ordered through booksellers or by contacting:

Balboa Press
A Division of Hay House
1663 Liberty Drive
Bloomington, IN 47403
www.balboapress.com
1 (877) 407-4847

ISBN: 978-1-5043-6532-1 (sc)
ISBN: 978-1-5043-6533-8 (e)

Print information available on the last page.

Balboa Press rev. date: 12/31/2016

BALBOA.
PRESS
A DIVISION OF HAY HOUSE

A bit about the author.........

Germaine Louise was born in the UK to a loving family that encouraged and supported her to excel at anything she wanted to do. She began writing at the age of 11, grew up dancing competitively and participated in musical theatre. Having the freedom to experience life in a way that felt like magic to her, led her to attend then teach performing arts programs.

Germaine could never imagine a world without her mother; then the unthinkable happened. When she was 26, her mother passed away. Feeling like her mother was always standing next to her, Germaine set off to the Rocky Mountains in Canada where her parents had always wanted to visit.

After working successfully in a corporate environment then owning her own business, Germaine knew she had a higher calling. She began traveling and sharing her '"magic" with every person she came in contact with, believing that everyone can achieve the freedom and happiness she experienced.

Following her heart is the only way she knows how to live. Be it travelling, writing or life coaching, she embraces every minute she gets and enjoys a very fulfilled life doing the things she loves. She is all about giving back to others in the best way she can. Her infectious energy is what captivates her audience and keeps them wanting to know all the secrets she possesses to be as happy as she is.

This book is simple. It shows how "one step at a time," you too can find the magic in yourself. Everyone not only deserves to be happy; we all have the ability to find this internal happiness. Find out for yourself.

Germaine encourages you to contact her to share your story. You can contact her at

30days@germainelouise.com.

Foreword

I want to thank my mother, father and my wonderful sister. Although my mother is no longer with me in the physical element, she taught me so much and gave me so many great qualities even though I didn't realize it at the time. She also showed me how to be honest with people and to never hold grudges. I continue to learn so much from her every day. My father I thank for his amazing energy and spirit. For I am who I am because of the way he is. He continues to show me that life is for living and a line I will always remember from him is, "You are a long time dead." So make the most of every second!

Then there is my amazing sister who was the motivation for me to write this book. She has been my go-to in life on so many occasions, and I couldn't wish for a better sister. I began the first draft back in 2012, and here we are now in 2016. I am so proud of myself for doing this with the help of Balboa Publishing. I also want to thank my brother-in-law for his amazing talent in photography. The photos for days 25 and 26 as well as my beautiful front cover were taken by him in Peregian, Australia. Another person who has impacted my life is my Nana White with all her mystical ways. It is amazing what we hear and learn so innocently as children and what in later life really shapes who we are.

I urge everyone out there to write their ideas down because like me you can get your start in life as a writer by contacting a publisher like Balboa. Someone once asked me,"What do you want to do in life?" My answer was, *"I want to make a difference and touch the lives of many."* So I hope this book helps to do that.

Follow your heart in all that you do. Dream big and never stop believing in magic. No matter how old you are, you're never to old for your dreams to come true.

Introduction

I think we either have, or all will reach a point in life where we feel a little down every now and again. To some it may happen more regularly than others, and that is fine; we are all different when it comes to our emotions. I feel what is important is how we allow ourselves to be affected by the everyday little stresses that come our way. In everything that we do, it is essentially how we deal with these things that allows us to overcome and get through them with ease.

I compiled this 30-day process in order to give you a little helping hand. It is really like a giant to-do list. I myself have been through times in my life when I craved a little order; only sometimes trying to motivate yourself to follow an agenda can be a challenge. I figured putting together a small handbook would be a great way to give people a little direction. Often all we need is a plan and a little inspiration, and that was my intention behind writing this.

The Process

There really are no set rules other than start at the beginning and work your way through all 30 days. It may be that you wish to start again immediately at the end in order to just keep yourself flowing.

I hope that following the process will help to bring that little bit of sunshine your way. I promise these are some of the most basic steps, but I am confident that by doing them, you will feel a sense of accomplishment and that your mind will feel more cleansed.

I encourage you to journal or make notes for your own reflection on the pages provided at the back of the book, as you carry out the steps. It could be beneficial if ever you want to look back on anything you may have noticed or felt during the process.

I am sure you'll find some steps more rewarding than others; the main thing to do is just start.

I hope you enjoy the journey

Germaine xo

LET'S GET YOU PREPARED!

Here are a couple of things you will need to go out and buy before the day itself so you are ready!

- A bundle of sage. (Anyplace that sells crystals, self-development books or tarot cards should have it.) I hope you won't feel any discomfort purchasing this. Burning sage really is a very old-fashioned spiritual ritual that helps to clear energies.

- Candles – Any kind will do. (Tea lights are always good if you are on a budget.)

- An essential oil that appeals to you. You can speak to the assistant in the store to get her advice if you are struggling or wondering about something specific. If you do have specific health ailments, then let the assistant know. Or else just do the blind test and go with what your senses are attracted to. My recommendations would be to choose something like citrus, lavender, jasmine or rosemary. See which one you like best as it's quite incredible how our noses sniff out different likes and dislikes for our own selves.

Overview of Steps

1. Sage
2. Telephone call
3. Candles
4. Declutter
5. Compliments
6. Flower day
7. Water
8. Pen to paper
9. Appointment
10. Hugging is loving
11. Give back
12. Time for a meet up with a friend
13. Beauty time
14. Dressing up
15. Relax and reflect
16. Book a trip
17. Spot of cleaning
18. Activity
19. Treat day
20. Favourite dinner
21. Pay that bill
22. Fresh air
23. Early to rise
24. Essential oil
25. Deep breathing
26. Expression of love
27. Forgiveness
28. Sing and dance
29. Chic and sexy
30. I love me

Day 1 – Lets get started by burning some sage

This was and still is used today by many spiritual groups for removing unwanted or negative energy. It may seem a little quirky, but I assure you it is nothing to feel worried about. I use sage quite often to help keep the energy around me positive. I would like you to light it at the end and let it burn so it gives off some smoke. Whilst it is burning, I want you to you walk through your bedroom, your entire home or even your office. Take deep breaths as you do and say out loud, or internally if there are people around, "I release all the energy that no longer serves me." This will help to clear out any negative energy in your surroundings. If you want to also circulate it around your body, that is good. Waving it in front of your 5 senses is a good start, EYES for what you see, EARS for what you hear, NOSE for what you smell, MOUTH for what you speak and your HANDS for what you touch.

Yeah!!! You completed your first one!!

Day 2 – A problem shared is a problem halved

Talking and sharing can have huge benefits on how you feel. As the old saying goes, "A problem shared is a problem halved." No one is saying you have to unleash everything that is going on inside you, but reaching out to someone you trust will always have a good effect. So today I would like you to call a good friend who you haven't spoken to in a while. Just having that connection with someone you know and care for, not to mention the good conversation will leave you feeling uplifted. The person you speak to will also feel uplifted from the communication too.

Day 3 – Today is the day to grab those candles a little TLC (tender loving care), is in store

Light them, put on some soft music and take a warm bath, a hot shower or a cold shower depending on your climate. Relax into your own little world and really appreciate the feeling of the water on your skin. Water can help us to cleanse the mind due to its calming element and the nature of its scientific effects. It can have an amazing impact on your soul, when you have a conscious awareness around it. So just immerse yourself and really allow the water to wash any tension(s) away. It won't hurt to speak out loud or internally when the water is running down you or is around you by saying, "Thank you for helping me to release anything I am holding."

Day 4 – It is time to organize and declutter

Find a closet, drawer or cupboard that needs some organizing. The aim is to clear it out and give it some order. Clutter in any form has a way of creating blocked energy and can make you or your space feel closed off. Decluttering creates an amazing energy and a feeling of openness. It also makes room for new things to come to you. It leaves you with a feeling of accomplishment. So once you have completed the task just sit and enjoy what you have achieved.

Day 5 – Compliment 3 people today

It might be something someone is wearing, or a colour that suits them. You might notice a pair of shoes a woman is wearing or a man's pleasant aftershave. Could be a co-worker, friend, family member or even someone you don't know who you just pass in the street. Watch as you start making compliments how good it makes you feel – and them too.

Day 6 – It's flower day

I want you to go and buy yourself a bunch of flowers today and put them somewhere in a prominent position – be it in your office, your home or even your bedroom.

Flowers are a gift from nature and bring colour and perfume to a room or place. The fact they are real also brings life to the area. Not to mention they are beautiful and so will make you smile every time you look at them.

It is lovely when you receive flowers from someone, so if it is an option, then grab a small bunch and give them to someone special too. It will have an amazing impact on their day.

Take a minute to stop and just look at them on a daily basis and see their natural beauty. You too are a like a flower if you look deep enough.

Day 7 – It is water time

Time to get you hydrated. I want you to drink 2 litres of water today. For flavour I recommend adding some freshly-squeezed lemon or lime to help alkaline you too. And yes, even though they are both acidic citrus fruits, when you drink them they have a great alkalizing effect on your body. A balanced alkaline level helps the body attain a state of harmony.

Drinking a good amount of water will help to fill you up and feel more energized. It is a great way to flush away those toxins, so after today, aim to keep it up.

Day 8 – Put pen to paper or fingers to laptop

Today I want you to write to someone. In the way of an email, or if you prefer, then do it the old-fashioned way and write a letter to anyone you have been wanting to get in touch with. I am sure if you think about it, there is a person who would love to hear from you. Maybe a little update on what you've been doing? It could be a friend or relative who doesn't live near you. We get so bombarded these days with bills and junk mail both in paper form and electronically that to get something personal is really quite a treat. I promise it will be worth the effort.

Day 9 – Book that appointment

Is there something you have been putting off? A doctor's check-up, visit to the dentist, an eye exam. Whatever it is, today is the day to address it and wipe it off that to-do list. It could be there is even more than 1, in which case make it a productive day and book them all. It could be just for you, or even you and your family. Just don't put it off anymore. Do it today and feel that relief knowing it is scheduled.

Day 10 – Hugging is loving

I want you to GIVE and GET 3 hugs today. Hugging is an incredible medicine. It allows us to give and release the "Love Drug" called oxytocin. Hugs also are a stimulant to the brain, so there is no passing this one up. Also aim to make the hug last 20 seconds. A quick 2-second hug doesn't allow for those chemicals and endorphins to take effect. If you have children or pets, then they are always an easy place to start. If not, maybe a friend, family member, a co-worker or a loving partner if you have one. Whatever it takes, just do it!!

Day 11 – Give back today

I would like you to make a donation. It can be money, clothes or even food. It doesn't have to be a lot - just an act of kindness that will leave you feeling wonderful! Pet shelters are always short on basics, like towels, old bedding etc., so that is always a good place to start. Or even schedule a quick trip to your local charity store to give them a few clothing items that you have cleared out from your closet. Maybe even donate a few old tins of food from your cupboard that you don't want/need anymore to a foodbank. Giving can feel like magic, and hopefully like most of these steps will and should leave you with that "feel good factor." Plus, I am a great believer that karma is always kind to you when you do these kinds of things.

Day 12 – Make time for a meet up

It could be a morning coffee, a lunch or maybe even a bite to eat in the evening if that is a better time for you. Work around your schedule, but make time to catch up with someone in person. Just as you first did in chatting with someone over the phone, now you take it one step further and get out of your house or working environment and go put yourself out into the world. Get the date in your diary, as it doesn't need to actually happen today, but once you have the plans confirmed, it is a date! If you can arrange it as quickly as today, then brilliant.

Day 13 – Beauty time

More TLC, as pampering all goes towards acts of self-love.

If you are in the position and have the funds, then please book a massage, facial, pedicure, manicure, something that allows you to relax for an hour. ME time is a great thing, and if you don't ever allow yourself some ME time, then some of these steps in this book will hopefully prompt you. Allow yourself at least 30 minutes for this.

If money won't allow you to go to a salon to do this, then set aside some time and find a way to DIY (do it yourself) at home. Try a face mask or hair mask from home ingredients. Try half an avocado, and a medium banana. Blend with a tablespoon of coconut oil, a dash of almond milk and mix it to a nice paste. Lather it on your hair and face and let it dry. Rinse off and feel wonderful! For a DIY massage, grab a tennis ball if you have one and rub it under the soles of your feet. Really get into those pressure points; it may hurt in places, but it is a great little exercise you can get into the habit of doing at night when you are watching the TV. It is very beneficial!

Day 14 - Dressing up time

It is time to get yourself looking smart and sassy. Whether it is the casual look, athletic look or the business look, I want you to MAKE AN EFFORT. If you're asking what that means, then just take a little extra care in getting ready. Wash and style your hair, wear a spray of perfume, add a necklace and maybe some earrings for extra effect. Ensure your clothes are clean and ironed if they are a fabric that benefits from being pressed. Finally, make sure your shoes are clean and polished. Walk out the door and know you look and feel like a million dollars. This is one of my favorites; I know it requires extra time, but it can honestly be very rewarding for the spirit and the soul. You never know; you might even get a few smiles or compliments from your transformation – in which case you might do it more often.

Day 15 – Relax and reflect

You're at the halfway point, so today I want you to just find time to SIT DOWN. Yes, you heard me, do nothing and answer to no one. No cleaning, no talking, no TV, no cell phone, no laptop. Just SIT and give yourself some **ME** time. Collect your thoughts and reflect on the things in your life. Aim to do it for at least 30 minutes. 60 minutes is even better. You might even find you snooze and take a nap... HURRAY... be kind to yourself and REST.

Ask yourself, "What do I want from life."

This is a good time to maybe take out a journal and document how you are feeling and how these processes are going for you. Please ensure you do the actual exercise first though, before you start to journal.

Day 16 – Early to rise

Set your alarm 10 minutes earlier than normal today (in fact, see if you can do it for the next 3 days). You don't have to get up out of bed; I just want you to lie there for 10 minutes and collect your thoughts. And please ensure you do not use this time to check your cell phone or emails. Ask yourself, *"What do I want to accomplish today? How do I want to feel today?"* Set one goal, write it down and think happy thoughts. Check back at the end of the day to see how you made out.

Day 17 - Time for a spot of cleaning

I want you to clean your bedroom from floor to ceiling today, including changing your bed sheets. Vacuum under your bed and all around the base boards. Give it a good dust and clear any rubbish or clutter that is building up. You will go to bed feeling fresh and ready for anything. Don't forget to take a quick shower before you jump in. Just lay there for a few minutes and recognise how it feels.

Can you feel that clarity and great energy all around you? It really is amazing how the energy around us has such an impact.

Day 18 – Time for some exercise or activity

I want you to go and find an exercise class to do today. It might be high impact or something more low impact like a yoga class. If you can't find anything then even a nice brisk walk will do the trick. Just devote 1 hour to doing an activity for yourself today. If you already work out, then maybe try doing something that you don't normally do. Swimming is always a good option because of the cleansing effect we get from the water (just as we did in step 3).

Day 19 – Today is a treat day for you! Time to do something nice for yourself

I would like you to go out and buy yourself something nice. It doesn't have to be anything expensive, just whatever you can afford. Perhaps a magazine, or a new book to read, maybe a nice new pair of shoes or a new purse or item of clothing. Treat yourself to a little personal gift and revel in that feeling of doing something nice just for you - an act of self-love. This can be a big step for those of you not used to self-nurturing. You are worthy to receive as well as give!

Day 20 – Prepare your favourite dinner

Make it something a little fancy, not something you make every week. Find that recipe that you have always wanted to try, or that you made and loved and have just never made again. Maybe you don't really ever cook so this could be quite the "MasterChef" challenge for you. It might be a romantic meal for YOU. Maybe you can invite a friend or friends, even a loved one or cook for your family. Just think about what you love to eat and cook it, make it a masterpiece

Day 21 – Let's pay that bill

This is similar to step 17; only this time it is not about an appointment but about a bill. Dig deep for this and see if you can find something to take care of. Maybe you owe a friend money, or could there be a naughty speeding fine lurking? Does your cell phone bill need to be paid or maybe a credit card or cable bill is due? Just find it, source it and get it paid. I am sure there will be something somewhere. If you are super in order and ahead of everything, then good for you. And if that is the case, then maybe find something and pay it early so you are a complete step ahead. Nothing like being prepared! This step can make one feel very liberated.

Day 22 – Let the fresh air in

Open all the windows and let the fresh air blow through your entire home, your office or wherever you happen to be. Sometimes we forget what nature gives us for free, especially when it is something that can also leave a place or ourselves feeling so cleansed. It will clean out the stagnant air within the home/area and will allow new air in – bringing a new freshness to all your surroundings. Take some slow deep breaths whilst you do it. Feel good with the new fresh-smelling air all around you.

Day 23 – Schedule/book a trip away

It could be a day trip somewhere, an overnight stay, a weekend away or might even be a vacation. It could be as small as a going out for a picnic and just taking a break, or even going to stay with a friend or family that doesn't live in the town where you live. Find someone who will commit to doing this with you if you can. If you have children, then is it possible you can make arrangements for them to be taken care of so you can have some ME time and a little break? Maybe you have a partner and can make it a little romantic getaway? If you are going it alone, then grab a good book to take with you and you will be just fine! Once it is booked or confirmed, YOU ARE GOING!!!!! It will give you something to focus on and get excited about.

Day 24 – Ok, time to grab your essential oil

This is a little step that I share with you because it is something that I have done from time to time on the recommendation of someone I worked closely with. The fragrance really is something that is special and unique to you. Wait until the end of your day, and when you get into bed tonight, rub a couple of drops into the soles of your feet. Lay there and inhale the scent and allow it to just drift over the space around you, thinking happy thoughts!

Day 25 – Deep breathing

Find a comfy place to sit or lay and take 10 deep breaths. Breathe in for 4, hold for 4 and exhale for 4. Take your time whilst doing this. Aim to just focus on your breath. If your brain gets busy, then just let the thoughts go. Deep breathing will help to clear and calm your energy. If you can try doing this twice a day, that would be great. Do it when you first wake and again before you sleep.

Day 26 – It is all about the love

My personal opinion? Love is the biggest and the best drug in the whole wide world. To give love and to be loved is about as good as it gets. So today, we are going to ensure the ones we love know it. Make a point of telling someone that you love them. This might sound easy, but for many it is not something you do on a daily basis. Maybe you live alone, and telling people you love them isn't something you get to do. If you live with a partner or have children, then maybe this is something you do, but do you really FEEL the meaning of the words? Anyway, the important thing is you find someone to tell, be it by text, email, or call if you cannot do it in person. Language is so powerful! Once again, sometimes we forget the things in life that are completely free and the impact they have.

Day 27 – Letter of forgiveness

I want you to write a letter of forgiveness. You do not have to send it; it is just a great way to release any supressed emotions, something that you are maybe still holding onto. It could be because a loved one has died or you have drifted apart from someone. The idea is that you forgive them for dying or leaving, and forgive yourself for how you may have felt or still feel or reacted. Maybe you've said/done something or behaved in a way towards someone that you wish you hadn't. Someone whose heart you've broken (and it could be from years ago), or someone who may have broken yours. WARNING: this may hurt and could bring a few tears, so ensure you are in a safe and quiet place when you do it. Just know that tears are a great release of toxins. It is far healthier to be rid of them, than to suppress them and hold on to negative feelings and emotions. The main thing here is that you are not only forgiving the other person involved for what happened, but you are actually forgiving yourself for feeling or acting as you did in a certain situation. Life does not judge you; it is YOU who does that. Either burn the letter after, or send it if you choose to. It will make you feel like a big weight has been lifted off your shoulders

Day 28 – Sing and dance

Find your favourite song or music video. It can be something recent or a blast from the past. Play it as loud as you can and ensure it is a song that makes you smile. We are going for a happy memory here, so play it over and over if you want to. Just dance and sing and get up and do your thing! No one is watching; remember how it made you feel and how it STILL makes you feel!!! If you break a sweat, keep going: releasing endorphins helps to make you feel better too.

Day 29 – It is time to heat things up a little

This is going to require a trip to the mall or a boutique shop. I would like you to go and treat yourself to some new lingerie. Pick something chic, a little fancy and sexy, and know you are buying it for YOU. If there is someone else in the picture, then it will be a double whammy. Anyway, I want you to take a shower, moisturize your skin, and then take your time to put it on. Obviously you then need to put clothes on over the top. Hold your head up high, put your shoulders back and walk down the street knowing you are a real sexy chick! If you don't live in a busy area, then go drive to a place where there are people. Just feel and know you are an absolute goddess when you are wearing the lingerie. You will be radiating and giving off so much sensual gorgeous energy, and people won't have a clue why (let that be your little secret). Just totally be 'Pretty Woman' for a day and work it baby: Work it!

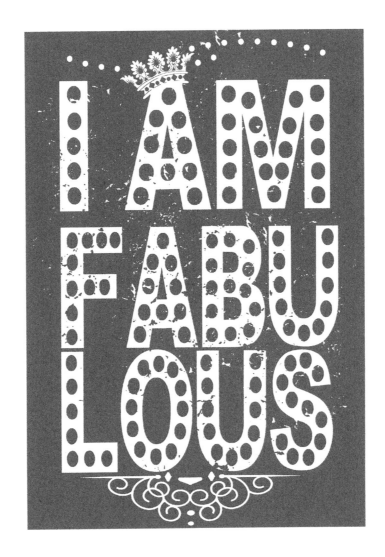

Day 30 – I love me

Finally, Look in the mirror and tell yourself out loud 10 times: **"I AM AMAZING, AND I AM SO THANKFUL FOR EVERYTHING THAT LIFE HAS SHOWN ME. I ACCEPT MYSELF FOR EXACTLY WHO I AM. I LOVE ME!"**

Well done - you did it!

Now is a perfect time to reflect on the steps you've taken, the ones you particularly enjoyed, as well as the ones you found more challenging. When you're ready, you may even wish to start the process again.

The great news is, by reading this book you've shown you love yourself—congratulations! I'd like to encourage your personal journey with a little more love from me.

At *germainelouise.com* you will find an abundance of free inspirational quotes and articles to brighten your day. Better yet, you can gain access to one-on-one coaching packages with yours truly. My loving gift to you is $50 towards your first package purchase, by simply mentioning your purchase to me. Because every step you take towards a positive, more fulfilling life counts.

Ask yourself, where do I want to be 6 months from now? One year from now? How do you want to feel in your day-to-day life? What challenges and successes lay before you?

These are tough questions, and I am *always* here to guide you.

Hugs,

Germaine
www.germainelouise.com
The Key to Igniting the Magic in You

Notes

Notes

Notes

Notes

Notes

Notes

_____

_____

_____

_____

_____

_____

_____

_____

_____

_____

_____

_____

_____

Notes

Notes

Notes

Notes

CPSIA information can be obtained
at www.ICGtesting.com
Printed in the USA
LVOW06s0707180117

521302LV00014B/105/P